I0003918

Ultimate Canva Manual

A Comprehensive Guide to Creating Stunning Graphics, Monetising Your Skills, and Improving Workplace Efficiency

Caleb Sterling Westwood

TABLE OF CONTENTS

Introduction

Why Canva?

In today's fast-paced digital world, visual content is more important than ever. Whether you're a small business owner, a content creator, a marketing professional, or simply someone who wants to design stunning visuals without spending hours learning complex software, Canva has become the go-to solution.

Canva is a powerful, user-friendly design platform that allows anyone—regardless of technical expertise—to create professional-looking graphics, presentations, social media posts, marketing materials, and more. Unlike traditional design tools like Adobe Photoshop or Illustrator, which require significant training and experience, Canva provides an intuitive drag-and-drop interface, making it accessible even to complete beginners.

Beyond ease of use, Canva offers a vast library of pre-designed templates, fonts, elements, and images, enabling users to quickly produce high-quality designs. Whether you need to design an Instagram post, a business logo, a YouTube thumbnail, or even an entire website, Canva provides everything you need in one place.

With its cloud-based accessibility, Canva allows users to create and edit designs on any device—desktop, tablet, or mobile—ensuring seamless workflow and collaboration. Additionally, Canva's free and Pro plans cater to different user needs, from casual users to professional designers and businesses looking to establish a strong visual brand identity.

This book will guide you from the absolute basics of using Canva to mastering its most advanced features, unlocking its full potential to help you create stunning visuals effortlessly.

Who This Book is For

This book is designed for anyone who wants to harness the full potential of Canva, regardless of their background or experience level. Whether you're just starting or already familiar with Canva but want to explore its advanced capabilities, this book will serve as a complete guide.

1. Beginners & Non-Designers

If you've never used Canva or any other design tool before, this book will introduce you to the basics in a simple, easy-to-follow manner. You'll learn how to navigate Canva's interface, use templates, and create designs from scratch without any prior experience in graphic design.

2. Small Business Owners & Entrepreneurs

Branding and marketing are essential for business success, and Canva allows small business owners to create high-quality marketing materials without the need for expensive designers. This book will show you how to create logos, business cards, promotional materials, and even social media content to elevate your brand.

3. Content Creators & Social Media Managers

If you create content for social media, you know the importance of eye-catching visuals. This book covers how to design engaging Instagram posts, YouTube thumbnails, Pinterest pins, LinkedIn banners, and more to help you grow your online presence and audience.

4. Educators & Students

Teachers, professors, and students can use Canva for presentations, infographics, lesson plans, and educational content. Canva's easy-to-use tools can help educators make learning materials more visually appealing and engaging.

5. Marketers & Business Professionals

Marketing professionals can streamline their workflow by creating consistent, branded content using Canva's powerful design tools. This book will guide you through creating ads, brochures, email marketing templates, and other business-related designs.

6. Freelancers & Aspiring Designers

If you're looking to monetize your design skills, Canva offers an excellent opportunity. Freelancers can create templates, design services, and digital products for clients. This book covers how to use Canva to build a design business, from creating and selling templates to offering graphic design services.

What You Will Learn

This book is structured to take you from a complete beginner to an advanced Canva user, unlocking all of its features and functions along the way. Here's a preview of what you'll gain from this book:

1. Mastering the Basics

- Setting up and navigating your Canva account
- Understanding the interface and tools
- Choosing between Free, Pro, and Team plans
- Learning basic design principles and best practices

2. Essential Design Tools and Features

- Using templates, elements, fonts, and color palettes
- Uploading and editing images
- Creating text effects, shadows, and transparency
- Understanding layers, grids, and alignment

3. Advanced Canva Features

- Utilizing Magic Resize for different platforms
- Removing backgrounds and enhancing images
- Creating animations and interactive designs
- Designing presentations and marketing materials

4. Content Creation for Different Purposes

- Designing for social media (Instagram, Facebook, YouTube, LinkedIn)
- Creating business materials (logos, flyers, business cards)
- Making personal projects (resumes, invitations, planners)

5. Collaboration and Workflow Optimization

- Sharing and collaborating with teams
- Organizing designs efficiently with folders

- Integrating Canva with external tools and platforms

6. Exporting and Publishing Your Designs

- Choosing the right file format (PNG, JPG, PDF, MP4)
- Printing designs with Canva Print
- Publishing directly to social media and websites

7. Monetizing Your Canva Skills

- Selling Canva templates
- Creating digital products and printables
- Offering freelance design services

8. Pro Tips and Tricks

- Fixing common design mistakes
- Using Canva shortcuts for efficiency
- Staying updated with new Canva features

By the end of this book, you will have mastered Canva's full potential, allowing you to create professional-quality designs effortlessly.

Whether you're using it for personal projects, business branding, or freelance work, Canva will become your go-to design tool.

Enjoy the journey!

Getting Started with Canva

Before you can begin designing with Canva, you need to understand how to set up an account, navigate the platform, and choose the right plan for your needs. This chapter will guide you through the essential steps to get started with Canva and ensure you are comfortable using its interface.

Creating a Canva Account

Canva is a web-based design tool, meaning you don't need to download any software—everything runs directly from your web browser or mobile app. Creating an account is free and takes just a few minutes.

Step 1: Accessing Canva

You can access Canva through:

- **Website**: https://www.canva.com
- **Mobile App**: Available on iOS and Android via the App Store or Google Play Store

Step 2: Signing Up

When you visit Canva's homepage, you'll be prompted to sign up. You can create an account using:

- **Email**: Enter your email address and create a password.
- **Google Account**: Sign up quickly using your Google credentials.
- **Facebook Account**: Link your Facebook profile for seamless login.
- **Apple ID**: Available for Apple users for quick sign-in.

Once you sign up, Canva will ask you about your intended use—whether you're a student, teacher, business, or personal user. This helps Canva tailor its recommendations, though it won't limit your access to features.

Step 3: Verifying Your Account

If you signed up using email, Canva will send you a verification link. Click the link in your email to activate your account.

Step 4: Completing Your Profile

After verification, Canva may ask for additional details, such as your name and preferences, to personalize your experience.

Once your account is set up, you're ready to explore the Canva dashboard!

Understanding the Dashboard

The Canva dashboard is the central hub where you access all your designs, templates, tools, and account settings. It's designed to be intuitive, so even beginners can navigate it easily.

Main Components of the Dashboard

1. **Home Tab**

   ○ This is the starting page whenever you log in.
   ○ Displays design suggestions based on your previous work and interests.
   ○ Features quick-access buttons for creating new designs.

2. **Templates Section**

   ○ Browse thousands of pre-made templates for presentations, social media, business cards, flyers, and more.

3. **Projects Tab**

- Stores all your previously created designs.
- Organizes files into folders for better management.
- Allows you to duplicate, edit, or share designs.

4. **Brand Hub (For Pro & Teams Users)**

- Lets you store brand assets like logos, fonts, and color palettes for consistency.

5. **Apps & Integrations**

- Connects Canva with third-party tools like Google Drive, Dropbox, and social media platforms.

6. **Trash**

- Deleted designs are stored here for 30 days before being permanently removed.

7. **Create a Design Button**

- Found at the top right of the dashboard.
- Clicking this opens a menu where you can choose the type of design you want to create.

8. **Account Settings & Profile**

- Click on your profile picture to access account settings, billing, and preferences.

By familiarizing yourself with the dashboard, you'll be able to quickly navigate Canva and access the tools you need for your designs.

Free vs. Pro vs. Teams: Which Plan to Choose

Canva offers different pricing plans based on your needs. Understanding the differences will help you decide which plan is best for you.

1. Canva Free Plan (Best for Casual Users & Beginners)

■ Features:

- Access to over **250,000 free templates**
- More than **1 million free images and graphics**
- Basic photo editing tools
- Download in standard formats (PNG, JPG, PDF)
- Limited storage (5GB)
- Basic collaboration features

⊘ Limitations:

- Limited access to premium images, fonts, and templates
- No background remover or Magic Resize
- No ability to save brand kits (logos, colors, fonts)

■ Who Should Use It?

- Individuals creating personal projects
- Casual users who don't need advanced features

2. Canva Pro Plan (Best for Professionals & Small Businesses)

💰 **Price:** Around $12.99/month or $119.99/year (varies by region)

⬛ **Features:**

- Everything in the Free plan, plus:
- **Over 100 million premium images, videos, and elements**
- Access to **over 600,000 premium templates**
- **Background remover** (AI-powered)
- **Magic Resize** (automatically resizes designs for different platforms)
- **Brand Kit** (store logos, fonts, and brand colors)
- **Content Planner** (schedule social media posts directly from Canva)
- Up to **1TB of cloud storage**
- Ability to **download designs with transparent backgrounds**

🚫 **Limitations:**

- Only allows **one user** per account (unless part of a team plan)

◼ Who Should Use It?

- Small business owners & entrepreneurs
- Social media managers & marketers
- Freelancers & designers who need premium content

---

3. Canva for Teams (Best for Companies & Collaboration)

💰 **Price:** Starts at $14.99/month for the first 5 users

◼ Features:

- Everything in Canva Pro, plus:
- Ability to add **multiple team members**
- Team collaboration with **real-time commenting & approvals**
- **Role-based permissions** (Admin, Template Designer, Member)

- Centralized **Brand Hub** for company-wide branding consistency

⊘ Limitations:

- More expensive than Pro if you're a solo user

◼ Who Should Use It?

- Businesses with marketing/design teams
- Teams that need real-time collaboration
- Agencies and large-scale content creators

Navigating the Interface

Once you've set up your Canva account and chosen a plan, it's time to explore the design editor.

1. The Toolbar (Left Sidebar)

The left sidebar houses the primary tools:

- **Templates** – Pre-designed layouts for various projects
- **Elements** – Graphics, icons, shapes, charts, and frames
- **Uploads** – Allows you to upload images, videos, and files
- **Text** – Add headings, body text, and stylized typography
- **Photos** – Access Canva's stock image library
- **Backgrounds** – Solid colors, gradients, and patterns
- **More** – Access integrations, apps, and premium features

2. The Canvas (Main Workspace)

- This is where you design and edit.
- Drag elements, resize, move, and customize your content.

3. The Top Menu Bar

- **File:** Save, make copies, and adjust page settings.

- **Resize:** Available in Pro, allows you to adjust dimensions quickly.
- **Undo/Redo:** Quickly reverse changes.
- **Download & Share:** Export your design or share it directly.

4. The Layers & Positioning Tools

- **Align & Group Elements:** Helps keep designs organized.
- **Transparency & Effects:** Adjust opacity and add text effects.
- **Locking & Duplicating Elements:** Prevent accidental movement and create copies easily.

Essential Tools and Features in Canva

Canva is packed with powerful tools that make design easy and accessible for everyone. Understanding its essential features will allow you to create professional-looking designs with minimal effort. This chapter will explore Canva's core tools, including templates, elements, text, images, and backgrounds, to help you maximize your creative potential.

Templates: Selecting and Customizing

What Are Templates?

Canva offers a vast collection of pre-designed templates tailored for different projects, including social media posts, presentations, business cards, flyers, resumes, and more. These templates provide a strong foundation, eliminating the need to start from scratch while allowing full customization.

How to Select a Template

1. **Log into Canva** and go to the homepage.
2. Use the search bar to type the design type (e.g., "Instagram Post," "Business Card," "YouTube Thumbnail").
3. Browse through the suggested templates.
4. Click on a template to preview it, then select **"Customize this template"** to start editing.

Customizing a Template

Once you've chosen a template, you can modify every element to match your style and purpose:

- **Editing Text:** Click on any text box to change the content, font, size, or color.
- **Replacing Images:** Drag and drop new images from the **Uploads** or **Photos** section.
- **Adjusting Colors:** Click on any design element and use the color picker to modify it.
- **Rearranging Elements:** Move, resize, rotate, or layer elements to achieve your desired look.

Tips for Using Templates Effectively

✔ Choose a template that closely aligns with your vision to minimize edits.

✔ Maintain consistency by sticking to your brand colors and fonts.

✔ Customize elements to make the design unique instead of using it as-is.

Elements: Shapes, Lines, and Graphics

What Are Elements?

Elements in Canva refer to design components such as shapes, icons, illustrations, stickers, charts, and frames. These elements enhance your design and add visual appeal.

Accessing Elements

1. Click on the **Elements** tab in the left sidebar.
2. Use the search bar to find specific elements (e.g., "arrows," "abstract shapes," "icons").
3. Browse categories like shapes, lines, stickers, and frames.

Types of Elements and Their Uses

- **Shapes:** Squares, circles, triangles, and customizable geometric figures for structuring designs.
- **Lines:** Straight, curved, dotted, and decorative lines for dividers or accents.
- **Icons and Graphics:** Searchable icons and illustrations to complement designs.

- **Frames:** Special elements that allow you to insert images inside different shapes.
- **Stickers & GIFs:** Animated elements perfect for social media content.

How to Customize Elements

- **Resize:** Click and drag the corners to adjust the size.
- **Change Color:** Click the color box in the toolbar to modify hues.
- **Rotate & Flip:** Use the rotate button or the **Flip** option to adjust positioning.
- **Transparency:** Adjust opacity for a subtle or layered effect.

Tips for Using Elements Effectively

✔ Use shapes to frame text or highlight important sections.

✔ Keep icon styles consistent (flat vs. outlined vs. 3D).

✔ Don't overcrowd designs with too many elements—keep it balanced.

Text: Fonts, Effects, and Pairing

Adding and Customizing Text

1. Click on the **Text** tab in the left panel.
2. Select **"Add a heading," "Add a subheading,"** or **"Add a body text."**
3. Type your text and use the top toolbar to customize fonts, size, color, spacing, and alignment.

Font Selection & Pairing

Fonts play a crucial role in design. Canva offers a variety of fonts categorized into:

- **Serif Fonts:** Classic and professional (e.g., Times New Roman, Merriweather).
- **Sans-Serif Fonts:** Modern and clean (e.g., Open Sans, Montserrat).
- **Script Fonts:** Elegant and decorative (e.g., Pacifico, Dancing Script).
- **Display Fonts:** Bold and unique for attention-grabbing headlines.

Font Pairing Tips

✔ Combine a bold headline font with a simple body font for contrast.

✔ Use no more than **two to three fonts** in a single design to maintain readability.

✔ Canva's **"Font Pairing"** tool suggests combinations that work well together.

Text Effects & Enhancements

Click on the **Effects** tab in the top toolbar to add creative styles to text:

- **Shadow:** Adds a soft or bold shadow behind text.
- **Lift:** Creates a raised 3D effect.
- **Glitch:** Distorted effect for a futuristic look.
- **Neon:** Glow effect, perfect for vibrant designs.
- **Curve:** Bends text into an arc.

Tips for Using Text Effectively

✔ Make headings larger and bold for easy readability.

✔ Use contrast between text and background

for clarity.

✔ Align text properly (centered, left, or justified) based on design needs.

Images: Uploads, Stock Photos, and Editing

Adding Images to Designs

You can insert images in Canva using:

- **Uploads:** Import your own images by dragging them into Canva.
- **Photos Library:** Access Canva's stock photo collection.
- **Image Links:** Paste an image link, and Canva will fetch it.

Customizing Images

- **Resize & Crop:** Click and drag the corners or use the **Crop** tool.
- **Adjust Brightness & Contrast:** Use the **Edit Image** panel to enhance images.

- **Apply Filters:** Add aesthetic effects like Black & White, Retro, or Warm.
- **Remove Background:** Available for **Canva Pro** users to make backgrounds transparent.

Tips for Using Images Effectively

✔ Use high-resolution images for a professional look.
✔ Avoid overcrowding—balance text and images.
✔ Use **frames** to crop images into specific shapes (circles, squares, etc.).

Backgrounds and Color Palettes

Choosing a Background

You can use:

- **Solid Colors:** Click the background and choose a custom color.

- **Gradients:** Pre-made smooth color transitions.
- **Patterns & Textures:** Built-in backgrounds such as marble, wood, or fabric.
- **Images as Backgrounds:** Upload your own or choose from Canva's stock library.

Color Palettes & Branding

Canva allows you to create and save color palettes to maintain consistency.

- **Click on any element and select the color tool** to apply a new color.
- **Use Canva's color combinations tool** to get pre-made palettes.
- **Pro users can set up Brand Kits** to save brand colors, fonts, and logos.

Tips for Using Backgrounds Effectively

✔ Light backgrounds work best for text-heavy designs.
✔ Dark or blurred backgrounds enhance text visibility.

✔ Use consistent color schemes to reinforce branding.

Designing Like a Pro in Canva

Canva's tools make it easy to create visually appealing designs, but to take your work to the next level, you need to apply professional design principles. This chapter covers essential design techniques, including foundational design principles, alignment tools, layering, and brand consistency. By mastering these techniques, you'll create more polished, balanced, and effective designs.

Understanding Design Principles

Great design is not just about creativity—it follows core principles that ensure clarity, harmony, and impact. Below are five essential design principles that will help you create professional-quality visuals in Canva.

1. Balance

Balance refers to the distribution of elements in a design to create a sense of stability.

- **Symmetrical Balance**: Elements are evenly spaced on both sides of the design.
- **Asymmetrical Balance**: Elements of different sizes and weights are arranged in a way that still feels balanced.
- **Radial Balance**: Elements radiate from a central point (e.g., circular designs).

- **Tip:** Use Canva's **alignment guides** to evenly space elements and create a visually balanced layout.

2. Contrast

Contrast is used to make elements stand out. It creates a visual hierarchy and draws attention to key areas.

- Use **dark text on a light background** or vice versa.
- Mix **bold fonts** with **thin fonts** for emphasis.
- Pair **large and small elements** to create a focal point.

 ◆ **Tip:** Canva's **Color Picker** helps you select contrasting colors for readability and impact.

3. Alignment

Alignment ensures that elements are positioned in an orderly, structured manner. Proper alignment makes a design look clean and professional.

- Align text to the **left, center, or right** for readability.
- Use **grids and guides** to position elements precisely.

- Maintain **consistent spacing** between design elements.

◆ **Tip:** Use Canva's **Position tool** to align elements quickly.

4. Hierarchy

Hierarchy refers to the arrangement of elements based on their importance. It guides the viewer's eye through the design in a logical way.

- **Larger fonts for headings**, smaller fonts for details.
- **Bold or color-highlighted text** to emphasize key information.
- **Spacing and placement** to differentiate elements.

◆ **Tip:** Use Canva's **Text Effects** to enhance hierarchy and make headings stand out.

5. Repetition & Consistency

Repetition reinforces branding and creates a cohesive look.

- Use the same **fonts, colors, and styles** throughout the design.
- Maintain **consistent spacing and alignment** in all pages of a presentation.
- Repeat **logos and brand colors** to establish brand identity.

♦ **Tip:** Canva's **Brand Kit (Pro feature)** allows you to save brand colors, fonts, and logos for easy application.

Using Grids, Guides, and Alignment Tools

Canva provides built-in tools to help you maintain structure and precision in your designs.

Grids: The Foundation of Good Layouts

Grids help organize elements, making them visually appealing and easier to read.

- Canva offers **pre-made grid layouts** under the **Elements tab**.

- You can use **multi-section grids** to arrange images and text in a structured way.
- Grids are useful for **collages, portfolios, or social media layouts**.

◆ **How to Use Grids in Canva:**

1. Click **Elements > Search "Grids"**
2. Select a grid layout and drag it onto the canvas.
3. Drag images or content into each grid section—it automatically snaps into place.

Guides & Rulers: Precision in Positioning

- Guides are **blue lines** that help position elements precisely.
- Rulers are **available under File > Show Rulers and Guides**.
- You can **drag guides** from the ruler to create custom alignment points.

◆ **How to Enable Guides in Canva:**

1. Click **File > View Settings > Show Guides**.
2. Drag a guide from the ruler to the canvas.
3. Align text and objects to maintain structure.

Alignment Tools: Keeping Everything Neat

Canva automatically helps you align elements by displaying **smart guides** when moving objects.

- **Auto-Snap:** Elements snap into place when aligned.
- **Position Tool:** Align objects **to the left, right, center, or distribute evenly**.
- **Spacing Adjustments:** Use the **Spacing tool** to evenly distribute elements.

- **Tip:** Press **Shift** while moving an object to keep it aligned horizontally or vertically.

Working with Layers and Transparency

Layering allows you to stack multiple elements in an orderly way, giving depth and structure to your design.

Understanding Layers in Canva

- **Elements are stacked** based on the order they were added.
- **The last element added is always on top** of others.
- You can rearrange layers using the **Position tool**.

How to Manage Layers in Canva

1. Click on an element.
2. Click **Position > Forward or Backward** to move it in the layer stack.
3. Lock important elements to prevent accidental movement.

◆ **Tip:** Hold **Ctrl (Windows) or Command (Mac)** while clicking multiple elements to move them together.

Adjusting Transparency for Depth and Effects

Transparency (Opacity) helps create subtle effects and blends elements together.

- Select an element and click **Transparency (checkerboard icon)**.
- Adjust the slider to make an element more or less visible.
- Use transparency on **backgrounds, overlays, or text boxes** to create professional effects.

 ◆ **Best Uses for Transparency:**

✔ **Watermarks** – Lower the opacity of a logo overlay.

✔ **Layering text over images** – Slightly fade the background for better readability.

✔ **Ghosted images** – Create soft, faded elements in the background.

Creating Consistency with Brand Kits

If you're designing for a business, consistency is key. Canva's **Brand Kit** (available in Pro) ensures all your designs match your brand identity.

Setting Up a Brand Kit

1. Go to **Brand Hub > Brand Kit** (Pro feature).
2. Upload your **logo** and **brand images**.
3. Set up **brand colors** by selecting a primary and secondary color palette.
4. Choose **brand fonts** and assign them to headings, subheadings, and body text.

Using Brand Kits for Consistency

- **Automatic Branding** – Apply your brand's colors and fonts with one click.
- **Pre-made Templates** – Customize templates while maintaining brand guidelines.
- **Collaboration** – Share the brand kit with team members to ensure uniform designs.

- ◆ **Tip:** If you don't have Canva Pro, create a **custom folder** with your brand assets to access them easily.

Advanced Features and Hidden Gems in Canva

Canva is more than just a simple design tool—it's packed with advanced features that can help you create professional, high-quality visuals with ease. Whether you're working on social media posts, presentations, branding materials, or videos, Canva's hidden gems can save time, boost creativity, and take your designs to the next level.

In this chapter, we will explore five powerful features:

1. **Magic Resize: Adapting Designs Instantly**
2. **Background Remover and Image Enhancements**
3. **Smart Mockups and Frames**
4. **Animations and Video Editing**
5. **Using AI-Powered Tools**

Let's dive in!

Magic Resize: Adapting Designs Instantly

One of Canva's most powerful tools is **Magic Resize**, which allows you to quickly adapt a design to different dimensions without having to redo everything manually.

What is Magic Resize?

Magic Resize is a **Canva Pro** feature that instantly resizes a design to fit various platforms, ensuring content looks perfect across multiple formats.

For example, if you create an **Instagram Post (1080x1080 px)** but later need it as a **Facebook Cover (820x312 px)**, Magic Resize automatically adjusts the elements to fit the new size.

How to Use Magic Resize

1. Open a design in Canva.
2. Click on the **Resize** button in the top toolbar.
3. Select one or multiple formats (e.g., YouTube Thumbnail, Instagram Story, LinkedIn Banner).
4. Click **Resize** or **Copy & Resize** to generate the new version.

◆ **Tip:** If the resized design looks misaligned, manually adjust elements using Canva's **positioning and alignment tools**.

Best Uses for Magic Resize

✔ Social media marketing (adapting posts for Instagram, Facebook, Twitter, LinkedIn).

✔ Repurposing content (converting blog graphics into Pinterest pins).

✔ Creating consistent branding across different platforms.

Background Remover and Image Enhancements

Background Remover: Creating Transparent Images

The **Background Remover** is another **Canva Pro** feature that lets you remove backgrounds from images with a single click—perfect for product photos, logos, and marketing materials.

How to Remove a Background

1. Select an image in your design.
2. Click on **Edit Image** in the top toolbar.
3. Choose **Background Remover** and wait for Canva to process the image.

4. Use the **Erase & Restore Brush** to fine-tune edges if needed.

◆ **Tip:** If you don't have Canva Pro, you can manually remove backgrounds using free online tools before uploading your image to Canva.

Image Enhancements: Adjusting Photos Like a Pro

Canva also provides built-in tools to improve image quality:

- **Brightness & Contrast** – Adjust lighting for a clearer image.
- **Blur & Sharpen** – Enhance focus or create depth.
- **Filters & Effects** – Apply artistic filters for a unique look.
- **Duotone & Color Mix** – Create dramatic color overlays.

◆ **Tip:** Experiment with **transparency** to blend images into backgrounds for a professional touch.

Best Uses for Background Remover & Image Enhancements

✔ Creating **product mockups** without distracting backgrounds.
✔ Designing **professional headshots** for LinkedIn or resumes.
✔ Removing busy backgrounds to make **text overlays** more readable.

Smart Mockups and Frames

Smart Mockups: Turning Designs into Real-World Products

Canva's **Smart Mockups** feature lets you place your designs onto realistic objects like **t-shirts, mugs, laptops, billboards, and packaging**.

How to Use Smart Mockups

1. Upload or create a design.
2. Click on **Edit Image > Smart Mockups**.

3. Browse mockup categories (technology, clothing, print, packaging).
4. Select a mockup and Canva will automatically apply your design.

◆ **Tip:** Use **Smart Mockups** to showcase branding on merchandise before production.

Frames: Creative Cropping & Unique Shapes

Frames allow you to insert images into **custom shapes** such as circles, letters, or abstract designs.

How to Use Frames

1. Go to **Elements** and search for **Frames**.
2. Drag a frame onto your canvas.
3. Drag an image into the frame—it will automatically crop to fit.

◆ **Tip:** Use **letter frames** to spell out words using images for an artistic effect.

Best Uses for Smart Mockups & Frames

✔ Branding presentations (showing logos on business cards and apparel).

✔ E-commerce product previews.

✔ Social media posts with **creative cropped images**.

Animations and Video Editing

Canva is not just for static graphics—it also offers animation and video editing tools to create **engaging motion graphics, slideshows, and marketing videos**.

Adding Animations to Your Design

Canva allows you to animate text, images, and entire slides to add movement and visual appeal.

How to Animate Elements

1. Select an element (text, image, or shape).
2. Click **Animate** from the top toolbar.
3. Choose from options like:
   - **Fade** (smooth transition)

- ○ **Rise** (elements float upward)
- ○ **Pan & Zoom** (dynamic movement)
- ○ **Bounce & Tumble** (fun, playful effects)

◆ **Tip:** Combine multiple animations for a professional look—e.g., fade-in text with a zoom effect on images.

Basic Video Editing in Canva

Canva also lets you create **video content** for social media, presentations, and marketing.

How to Edit Videos in Canva

1. Click **Create a Design > Video** and choose a template.
2. Upload or select a stock video.
3. Trim clips, add transitions, and insert music or voiceovers.
4. Export in MP4 format.

◆ **Tip:** Use **animated stickers & overlays** to make videos more engaging.

Best Uses for Animations & Video Editing

✔ Instagram Stories & TikTok videos.
✔ Business presentations & YouTube intros.
✔ Promotional ads & motion graphics.

Using AI-Powered Tools

Canva has introduced several **AI-powered features** that make designing even easier.

1. Magic Write (AI Copywriting)

Canva's **Magic Write** helps generate text for social media posts, blog headers, product descriptions, and marketing materials.

- ◆ **How to Use Magic Write:**

  1. Open a design and select a text box.
  2. Click **Apps** > **Magic Write** and enter a prompt (e.g., "Write a catchy Instagram caption for a fashion brand").

3. Canva generates text suggestions instantly.

2. Text-to-Image (AI Image Generator)

Canva's **Text-to-Image** AI allows you to create unique images from written descriptions.

- **How to Use Text-to-Image:**

  1. Go to **Apps > Text to Image**.
  2. Enter a description (e.g., "a futuristic city with neon lights").
  3. Canva generates an AI-powered image for you to use.

3. AI-Powered Layouts

Canva's **Layouts** feature automatically suggests design improvements to enhance visual appeal.

- **Tip:** If you're stuck on a design, click **"Suggestions"** to see AI-powered layout recommendations.

Best Uses for AI Tools

✔ Quickly generating **social media captions & content ideas**.

✔ Creating **unique AI-generated images** for marketing materials.

✔ Improving **design layouts with smart AI recommendations**.

Designing for Different Purposes in Canva

Canva is an incredibly versatile design tool that caters to a wide range of creative needs. Whether you're crafting **social media graphics, business materials, marketing collateral, personal projects, or website designs**, Canva offers pre-designed templates, customization tools, and professional elements to make your work stand out.

In this chapter, we will explore how to design for:

1. **Social Media Graphics (Instagram, Facebook, YouTube, LinkedIn)**
2. **Business Materials (Logos, Business Cards, Presentations)**
3. **Marketing Collaterals (Flyers, Brochures, Posters)**
4. **Personal Projects (Invitations, Resumes, Planners)**
5. **Websites and Landing Pages**

Social Media Graphics

Social media is a highly visual platform, and **eye-catching graphics** can make all the difference in engagement, branding, and conversions. Canva provides ready-made templates for various platforms, ensuring that your designs are the perfect size and format.

1. Instagram Graphics

Instagram is one of the most visual social platforms, and Canva supports multiple content types:

✔ **Instagram Posts (1080x1080 px)** – Ideal for product promotions, quotes, and branding.

✔ **Instagram Stories (1080x1920 px)** – Great for time-sensitive announcements.

✔ **Instagram Reels Covers** – Custom covers maintain brand consistency.

- ◆ **Tips for Instagram Designs:**

  - Use **bold fonts** and **high-contrast colors** for better readability.
  - Keep text minimal—let visuals do most of the talking.
  - Utilize Canva's **animation tools** to make static posts more dynamic.

2. Facebook Graphics

Canva offers templates for Facebook posts, event covers, and ads.

✔ **Facebook Posts (1200x630 px)** – Standard news feed images.

✔ **Facebook Covers (820x312 px)** – Banners for profiles and business pages.

✔ **Facebook Ads** – Optimized templates for different ad placements.

- ◆ **Tips for Facebook Designs:**

  - Use **attention-grabbing headlines** and **brand colors** for consistency.
  - Ensure **text takes up less than 20%** of the image for better ad performance.
  - Keep designs **mobile-friendly**, as most users access Facebook via smartphones.

3. YouTube Thumbnails & Channel Art

YouTube thumbnails **influence click-through rates**, while channel art helps establish branding.
✔ **Thumbnails (1280x720 px, 16:9 ratio)** – Eye-catching, bold, and visually clear.
✔ **Channel Art (2560x1440 px)** – Ensure important elements stay in the **safe zone** (1546x423 px).

- ◆ **Tips for YouTube Graphics:**

  - Use **bold, readable text** and **contrasting colors**.

- Feature a **face or main subject** to grab attention.
- Keep thumbnails **consistent** in style and branding.

4. LinkedIn Banners & Posts

LinkedIn graphics should be **professional and polished** to enhance credibility.

✔ **LinkedIn Banner (1584x396 px)** – Clean and minimal, featuring company branding.

✔ **LinkedIn Post (1200x627 px)** – Engaging visuals for career-related content.

◆ **Tips for LinkedIn Designs:**

- Stick to **neutral or corporate color palettes**.
- Use **minimalist, professional fonts** (e.g., Montserrat, Lato).
- Avoid clutter—less is more in professional settings.

Business Materials

1. Logos

Logos define a brand's identity and should be simple yet memorable. Canva provides:

✔ **Logo Templates** – Customizable to match your brand.

✔ **Brand Kits (Pro Feature)** – Save logo, fonts, and color palette for consistency.

♦ **Tips for Logo Design:**

- Stick to **one or two colors** for versatility.
- Ensure the logo works in **both color and black & white**.
- Choose **scalable** designs that look good in all sizes.

2. Business Cards

Business cards should be **clean, readable, and on-brand**. Canva's standard business card size is **3.5x2 inches**.

♦ **Tips for Business Card Designs:**

- Use **high-contrast text** for readability.

- Include essential information (name, contact, website, social links).
- Keep the design **simple and uncluttered**.

3. Presentations

Canva's **presentation templates** are perfect for **business pitches, training materials, and reports**.

- ◆ **Tips for Presentations:**

  - Use **bullet points** instead of long paragraphs.
  - Keep **fonts large (24pt minimum)** for readability.
  - Utilize **charts and infographics** to make data visually engaging.

Marketing Collaterals

1. Flyers

Flyers are **great for promotions, sales, and event announcements**. Canva offers templates in **A4 and US Letter sizes**.

- ◆ **Tips for Flyer Designs:**

  - Use **one striking image** or graphic as the focal point.
  - Keep text **concise**—only include key details.
  - Utilize **contrast and bold fonts** to emphasize offers.

2. Brochures

Brochures provide detailed product or company information. Canva supports **bifold and trifold formats**.

- ◆ **Tips for Brochure Designs:**

  - Use **sections and columns** for easy reading.
  - Include **high-quality images** to enhance credibility.

- Maintain **brand colors and fonts** throughout.

3. Posters

Posters are designed for **maximum visibility** and should grab attention quickly.

- ◆ **Tips for Poster Designs:**

  - Use **large, bold headlines** to draw focus.
  - Maintain a **strong visual hierarchy** (headline > image > details).
  - Ensure text is readable **from a distance**.

Personal Projects

1. Invitations

Canva provides beautiful templates for **weddings, birthdays, and corporate events**.

- ◆ **Tips for Invitation Designs:**

- Match the theme with **elegant fonts and colors**.
- Use **decorative elements** like borders or flourishes.
- Keep text **centered** for a polished look.

2. Resumes

Stand out with a professional, modern resume template.

- ◆ **Tips for Resume Designs:**

  - Use **easy-to-read fonts** like Lato or Open Sans.
  - Keep it **one page** (unless applying for an academic role).
  - Highlight **skills and achievements** with icons or graphs.

3. Planners & Journals

Canva allows you to create **custom planners, habit trackers, and bullet journals**.

- ◆ **Tips for Planner Designs:**

- Use **grid or table layouts** for structured designs.
- Include **checklists, trackers, and goal sections**.
- Keep **color coding** for organization.

Websites and Landing Pages

Canva now offers **basic website-building tools**, perfect for portfolios, event pages, and simple business sites.

1. Designing a Website in Canva

✔ Choose a **website template** (single-page or multipage).
✔ Customize text, images, and colors.
✔ Publish as a **Canva-hosted site** or export as an image.

- ◆ **Tips for Website Designs:**

  - Keep a **clean, modern layout**.

- Use **consistent branding** with logos and fonts.
- Ensure the design is **mobile-friendly**.

Collaboration and Workflow Optimization in Canva

Canva isn't just a design tool—it's a powerful **collaboration platform** that allows individuals and teams to work efficiently on projects in real time. Whether you're a business owner, marketer, educator, or designer, Canva offers features that streamline teamwork, making it easier to share, edit, and organize designs while integrating with other platforms.

In this chapter, we'll cover:

1. **Sharing and Collaborating in Teams**
2. **Commenting and Real-Time Edits**
3. **Organizing Files and Folders Efficiently**
4. **Integrating Canva with Other Platforms**

---

1. Sharing and Collaborating in Teams

Canva allows seamless collaboration by enabling multiple users to **view, edit, and comment** on designs in real time. This feature is especially useful for **marketing teams, social media managers, educators, and businesses** that need to work on shared projects.

Setting Up Team Collaboration in Canva

To collaborate efficiently, you need to create a **Canva Team** (available in **Canva Free, Pro, and Teams** plans).

Creating a Team in Canva

1. Click on your profile picture in the top-right corner of Canva.
2. Select **"Create a Team"** or go to Canva Teams.
3. Enter a team name and invite members via email or link.
4. Assign roles to team members:
   - **Administrator** – Full control over designs and team settings.
   - **Template Designer** – Can create templates for the team.
   - **Member** – Can edit and contribute to designs.

◆ **Tip:** For large organizations, use **Canva for Teams**, which offers **brand control, approval workflows, and shared asset libraries**.

Sharing Designs with Individuals

If you don't have a team set up, you can still share designs with others.

How to Share a Design

1. Open your design and click **Share** in the top-right corner.
2. Enter an email address or generate a **shareable link**.
3. Choose a permission level:
   - **Can View** – The recipient can see the design but not edit it.
   - **Can Comment** – The recipient can leave feedback but not make changes.
   - **Can Edit** – The recipient can edit the design.

- **Tip:** You can also set **password protection** and **expiration dates** for shared links (available in Canva Pro).

---

2. Commenting and Real-Time Edits

Canva's **real-time collaboration** and **commenting system** make teamwork smoother.

Adding and Managing Comments

1. Open a shared design.
2. Click on an element or specific section of the design.
3. Select the **Comment** icon (speech bubble).
4. Type your message and mention teammates using **@username**.
5. Click **Post** to add the comment.

◆ **Tip:** Use comments to provide feedback, request changes, or discuss design choices.

Resolving Comments

- Once feedback has been addressed, click **Resolve** to remove the comment.
- Resolved comments are stored for reference and can be reopened if needed.

Live Editing and Version Control

Canva allows multiple users to edit a design simultaneously. Changes appear in **real time**, ensuring teams stay aligned.

◆ **Tip:** If you need to restore a previous version of a design, use **Canva's Version History** (available in Canva Pro).

---

3. Organizing Files and Folders Efficiently

As your projects grow, keeping your Canva workspace **organized** is essential for productivity.

Creating and Managing Folders

1. Go to **Projects** in the left-hand panel.
2. Click **Create Folder** and name it appropriately (e.g., "Social Media Graphics").
3. Drag and drop designs into folders or use the **Move To** option.
4. Share folders with your team to ensure **easy access to assets**.

◆ **Tip:** Canva Pro users can create **unlimited folders** while free users are limited to a few.

Using Tags and Search for Quick Access

- Add **tags** to designs (e.g., "Instagram," "Flyers," "Branding") for easy searching.
- Use the **search bar** in the Projects tab to quickly find past designs.

Saving and Reusing Templates

- Convert frequently used designs into **team templates** for consistent branding.
- Save branded elements (logos, fonts, colors) in a **Brand Kit** (available in Canva Pro).

- ◆ **Tip:** If you manage multiple brands, set up **separate brand kits** to maintain consistency across different projects.

---

4. Integrating Canva with Other Platforms

Canva integrates seamlessly with various tools and platforms, making it even more efficient for workflow management.

Social Media Integrations

You can publish designs directly to:

✔ **Facebook & Instagram** – Schedule or post directly.

✔ **LinkedIn & Twitter** – Upload graphics effortlessly.

✔ **Pinterest** – Create engaging pins instantly.

◆ **Tip:** Use **Canva's Content Planner** (Pro feature) to schedule posts in advance.

Cloud Storage Integrations

Save and access designs easily with:

✔ **Google Drive**
✔ **Dropbox**
✔ **OneDrive**

◆ **Tip:** Upload assets directly from cloud storage into Canva designs.

Presentation & Document Tools

✔ **Google Slides & PowerPoint** – Export presentations in PPT format.

✔ **Microsoft Word** – Import Canva graphics into reports.

- **Tip:** Use **Canva Presentations** with "Presenter View" for live, interactive sessions.

E-Commerce & Website Integrations

✔ **Shopify & Etsy** – Create branded store banners.
✔ **WordPress** – Design blog images and upload seamlessly.
✔ **Canva Websites** – Build a one-page site directly in Canva.

Email & Marketing Integrations

✔ **Mailchimp** – Design email newsletters.
✔ **HubSpot & Constant Contact** – Import Canva visuals for campaigns.

- **Tip:** Canva offers **QR code generation** for easy linking to websites or landing pages.

Exporting and Publishing Your Designs in Canva

Once you've created a stunning design in Canva, the next step is to **export, print, or publish it** in the right format for your intended use. Whether you need a **high-resolution print**, a **social media post**, or an **animated video**, Canva provides multiple export and sharing options to ensure your design reaches its audience in the best possible quality.

In this chapter, we'll explore:

1. **Downloading in Different Formats (PNG, JPG, PDF, MP4, SVG)**

2. **Printing with Canva Print**
3. **Sharing Directly to Social Media**
4. **Embedding Designs on Websites**

---

1. Downloading in Different Formats (PNG, JPG, PDF, MP4, SVG)

How to Download Your Canva Design

1. Click the **Share** button in the top-right corner of Canva.
2. Select **Download**.
3. Choose the appropriate **file type**.
4. Adjust additional settings (e.g., resolution, transparency, page selection).
5. Click **Download** to save the file to your device.

Understanding File Formats and When to Use Them

PNG (Portable Network Graphics)

✔ Best for: **High-quality images, transparent backgrounds, logos, social media posts**
✔ Features:

- Supports **transparent backgrounds** (great for overlays, logos).
- Retains high quality without compression.

◆ **Tip:** If your design has a **transparent background**, check the **"Transparent Background"** box before downloading (Pro feature).

JPG (Joint Photographic Experts Group)

✔ Best for: **Web images, photographs, email attachments**
✔ Features:

- Compressed file size (loads faster on websites).
- Ideal for sharing on social media without large file sizes.

◆ **Tip:** Use JPG if you need a **smaller file size with decent quality**.

PDF (Portable Document Format)

✔ Best for: **Documents, print-ready designs, e-books, brochures, presentations**
✔ Features:

- **PDF Standard** – Smaller file size, optimized for web and screen viewing.
- **PDF Print** – High-quality version for professional printing (supports CMYK color profiles).

♦ **Tip:** For professional printing, use **"PDF Print"** with **crop marks and bleed** enabled.

MP4 (Video Format)

✔ Best for: **Animations, video presentations, social media stories**
✔ Features:

- Exports **animated** designs with smooth motion.
- High-quality video output for platforms like Instagram Reels, TikTok, and YouTube.

◆ **Tip:** If your design includes **animations or motion graphics**, use **MP4** instead of GIF for better quality.

SVG (Scalable Vector Graphics) – Canva Pro Only

✔ Best for: **Logos, icons, scalable vector images**
✔ Features:

- Retains quality at **any size** without pixelation.
- Editable in vector design software like **Adobe Illustrator**.

◆ **Tip:** Use SVG for **branding assets** (logos, icons) that need resizing without loss of quality.

---

2. Printing with Canva Print

Canva offers a **print-on-demand service** called **Canva Print**, allowing users to order high-quality prints directly from the platform.

How to Print with Canva Print

1. Click **Share** > **Print your design**.
2. Select the **print format** (e.g., business cards, posters, flyers, T-shirts).
3. Choose **paper type, finish, and quantity**.
4. Preview the design and adjust **crop marks & bleed** if needed.
5. Place your order, and Canva will ship the prints to your address.

Types of Prints Available

✔ **Business Cards** – Double-sided, premium stock options.

✔ **Posters & Flyers** – Glossy or matte finish for marketing materials.

✔ **T-Shirts & Hoodies** – Custom apparel with your design.

✔ **Invitations & Greeting Cards** – High-quality cardstock prints.

◆ **Tip:** Always use **PDF Print** with **300 DPI resolution** to ensure sharp, professional-quality prints.

---

3. Sharing Directly to Social Media

Canva allows you to **post directly to social media** without needing to download your design first.

How to Share on Social Media

1. Click **Share > Share on Social Media**.
2. Choose a platform: **Facebook, Instagram, LinkedIn, Twitter, Pinterest, TikTok, etc.**
3. Add a caption, hashtags, and any additional details.
4. Click **Post Now** or **Schedule** for later (Pro feature).

Platforms You Can Post to Directly

✔ **Facebook & Instagram** – Feed posts, Stories, and Reels.
✔ **LinkedIn & Twitter** – Business and professional content.
✔ **Pinterest** – High-quality pin uploads for

visual marketing.

✔ **TikTok & YouTube** – Video content with MP4 format.

♦ **Tip:** If you manage multiple social media accounts, use **Canva's Content Planner** (Pro feature) to schedule posts in advance.

---

4. Embedding Designs on Websites

Canva provides an **embed code** that allows you to showcase designs **directly on websites, blogs, or presentations** without downloading the file.

How to Embed a Canva Design

1. Click **Share > More > Embed**.
2. Copy the **HTML embed code**.
3. Paste it into your website, blog post, or online portfolio.

Where to Embed Canva Designs

✔ **WordPress & Blog Posts** – Insert infographics, banners, and visuals.

✔ **Online Portfolios** – Showcase work dynamically.

✔ **Email Newsletters** – Embed engaging graphics.

◆ **Tip: Any changes you make in Canva will automatically update the embedded design**, making it a great option for live updates.

Monetizing Your Canva Skills: Turning Creativity into Income

Canva is more than just a design tool—it's an opportunity to **build a profitable business** using your creativity. Whether you want to sell **templates, digital products, or design services**, Canva provides an accessible way to earn income. This chapter explores multiple ways to **monetize your Canva skills**, from selling pre-made designs to offering high-value freelance services.

In this chapter, we will cover:

1. **Selling Canva Templates**
2. **Creating and Selling Digital Products**
3. **Offering Freelance Canva Services**
4. **Growing a Design-Based Business**

---

1. Selling Canva Templates

One of the most profitable ways to monetize Canva is by **selling templates** to businesses, content creators, and entrepreneurs. With the rise of **digital marketing and branding**, people are constantly looking for **ready-made, customizable designs** that save time.

What Are Canva Templates?

A **Canva template** is a pre-designed file that customers can edit using their **own text, images, and branding**. Templates can be used for:

✔ Social media posts (Instagram, Facebook, Pinterest, LinkedIn)

✔ Business branding (logos, business cards, presentations)

✔ Marketing materials (flyers, brochures, media kits)

✔ Personal projects (resumes, planners, invitations)

How to Create Sellable Canva Templates

1. **Research Market Demand**

   - Browse **Etsy, Creative Market, and Envato Elements** to see trending templates.
   - Identify niche-specific needs (e.g., real estate, coaching, beauty brands).

2. **Design High-Quality Templates**

   - Use **professional layouts, color palettes, and fonts**.
   - Keep elements **editable and well-organized**.

- ○ Ensure **mobile and desktop compatibility**.
3. **Prepare Templates for Sale**

   - ○ **Save as a Canva Template Link** (Share > Template Link).
   - ○ Create a **PDF delivery file** with the template link and usage instructions.
4. **Choose a Selling Platform**

   - ○ **Etsy** – Best for selling pre-made digital templates.
   - ○ **Creative Market** – Ideal for premium design assets.
   - ○ **Gumroad** – Great for digital downloads with flexible pricing.
   - ○ **Your Own Website** – Sell templates directly with Shopify or WooCommerce.

Pricing Canva Templates

✔ Single-use templates: **$5 - $25**
✔ Bundle packs: **$30 - $100**
✔ Exclusive custom templates: **$100+**

◆ **Tip:** Selling **bundles of templates** (e.g., "100 Instagram Post Templates") increases value and profit!

---

2. Creating and Selling Digital Products

Beyond templates, you can use Canva to design **digital products** that people are willing to pay for. These products are **easy to create, require no inventory, and offer passive income** opportunities.

Best Digital Products to Sell

✔ **Planners & Printables** – Daily planners, wedding planners, budget trackers
✔ **Workbooks & E-books** – Online course materials, business guides
✔ **Social Media Kits** – Instagram highlight covers, Facebook banners

✔ **Lead Magnets** – Freebies to help businesses grow their email lists
✔ **Wall Art & Posters** – Printable home decor

How to Sell Digital Products Online

1. **Design your product in Canva**

   o Choose an appropriate size and format (e.g., PDF for printables, PNG for graphics).

2. **Set Up an Online Store**

   o Sell on **Etsy, Shopify, Gumroad, or Sellfy**.
   o Use a **landing page** to promote digital products.

3. **Market Your Products**

   o Use **Pinterest and Instagram** to showcase your designs.
   o Offer **discounts, freebies, and bundle deals** to attract buyers.

◆ **Tip:** Combine multiple products into a "**Mega Bundle**" to increase value and pricing.

---

3. Offering Freelance Canva Services

If you prefer **working directly with clients**, offering **freelance design services** is a lucrative way to monetize Canva. Many businesses and entrepreneurs **lack design skills** and are willing to pay for high-quality visuals.

What Canva Services Can You Offer?

✔ **Social Media Branding** – Custom Instagram posts, Facebook covers, LinkedIn banners
✔ **Logo & Branding Kits** – Unique logo designs, business cards, brand color palettes
✔ **Presentation Design** – Pitch decks, corporate presentations
✔ **Marketing Materials** – Flyers, brochures, e-books, lead magnets
✔ **Video Editing** – Short promotional videos, animated ads

How to Find Clients

1. Freelance Platforms

- **Fiverr** – Offer affordable Canva services to build your portfolio.
- **Upwork** – Work with high-paying business clients.
- **PeoplePerHour** – A great place for finding short-term design projects.

2. Social Media & Networking

- Promote your work on **Instagram, LinkedIn, and Pinterest**.
- Join **Facebook groups** for entrepreneurs who need design services.
- Offer **free or discounted** designs to attract new clients.

3. Cold Outreach & Word-of-Mouth

- Reach out to small business owners and offer **branding packages**.

○ Get **referrals from satisfied clients**.

Pricing Your Canva Services

✔ Social media graphics package: **$50 - $200**
✔ Branding & logo package: **$300 - $1000**
✔ Presentation design: **$150 - $500**
✔ Marketing material design: **$100 - $500**

◆ **Tip: Offer subscription-based design services** (e.g., "$500/month for unlimited graphics") to generate **recurring income**.

---

4. Growing a Design-Based Business

If you want to scale beyond freelancing, consider turning your **Canva skills into a full-fledged design business**.

How to Build a Canva-Based Business

✔ **Create an Agency** – Hire a team to handle multiple design clients.

✔ **Offer Coaching & Courses** – Teach others how to use Canva for business.

✔ **License Your Designs** – Sell designs on stock websites like **Envato Elements**.

✔ **Start a YouTube Channel or Blog** – Share Canva tutorials and earn through ads, sponsorships, and affiliate marketing.

Expanding Your Income Streams

- **Affiliate Marketing** – Earn commissions by promoting **Canva Pro** through Canva's affiliate program.
- **Subscription-Based Content** – Offer exclusive templates on **Patreon or Ko-fi**.
- **Corporate Training** – Teach Canva workshops for businesses and charge a **premium fee**.

Troubleshooting and Pro Tips: Mastering Canva Like a Pro

Even the most skilled designers encounter challenges when using Canva. Whether you're dealing with **alignment issues, blurry images, slow workflow, or missing features**, knowing how to troubleshoot common problems can save you time and frustration. Additionally, learning **lesser-known shortcuts and hacks** will help you **speed up your workflow and maximize your efficiency**.

This chapter covers:

1. **Fixing Common Design Mistakes**
2. **Speeding Up Your Workflow**
3. **Lesser-Known Shortcuts and Hacks**
4. **Staying Updated with Canva's Latest Features**

---

1. Fixing Common Design Mistakes

While Canva makes designing easier, **beginners and even advanced users** often make mistakes that affect the final product. Below are some of the most common errors and how to fix them.

Mistake #1: Blurry or Pixelated Images

Problem: Your downloaded image looks blurry, especially when resized or printed.
Solution:
✔ **Use high-resolution images** (at least 300 DPI for print).
✔ **Download in the correct format**:

- For web: PNG (for crisp graphics) or JPG (for smaller file size).
- For print: PDF Print (to maintain high resolution).

✔ **Avoid enlarging small images**—if an image is too small, it will lose quality when stretched.

Mistake #2: Poor Font Pairing and Readability Issues

Problem: The text in your design is hard to read or doesn't look professional.

Solution:

✔ Use **contrasting font pairings** (e.g., bold headlines with simple body text).

✔ Maintain **proper text hierarchy**: Headings should be larger and bolder than subheadings.

✔ Avoid **overusing script fonts** (they look elegant but can be difficult to read).

- **Pro Tip:** A great font pairing example:

  - Heading: **Montserrat Bold**
  - Subheading: **Open Sans**

- Body text: **Lora Regular**

Mistake #3: Unbalanced Layouts and Crowded Designs

Problem: Your design looks cluttered, making it visually overwhelming.

Solution:

✔ Use **white space** (empty areas) to avoid overcrowding.

✔ Align elements **properly** using Canva's grid and alignment tools.

✔ Stick to **3-5 colors** in your design for a clean, cohesive look.

- **Pro Tip:** Use the **"Tidy Up"** button (Position > Tidy Up) to align multiple elements perfectly.

Mistake #4: Inconsistent Branding in Designs

Problem: Colors, fonts, and elements are inconsistent across different designs.

Solution:

✔ Use **Canva's Brand Kit** (Pro feature) to save and apply consistent brand colors, fonts, and logos.

✔ Stick to **one or two primary fonts** across all designs.

✔ Use **pre-made templates** for consistency in social media posts and marketing materials.

---

2. Speeding Up Your Workflow

To **save time and design faster**, here are **workflow hacks** to boost efficiency.

1. Use Pre-Made Templates to Start Quickly

Instead of designing from scratch, **start with a template** and customize it. Canva provides thousands of **professional templates** for social media, presentations, and marketing materials.

2. Create Reusable Design Elements

✔ Save frequently used elements (logos, icons, brand colors) to **"Folders"** in Canva.

✔ Use the **Brand Kit (Pro feature)** to store brand fonts and colors.

✔ Duplicate and repurpose old designs instead of creating new ones from scratch.

3. Organize Your Canva Projects

✔ Use **folders** to categorize designs (e.g., Social Media, Business, Marketing).
✔ Name files **clearly** (e.g., "Instagram Post - Spring Sale" instead of "Untitled Design").
✔ Archive old projects to **declutter your workspace**.

4. Master Canva's Drag-and-Drop Features

✔ Drag images, text, and elements into **placeholders** for instant replacement.
✔ Drag files directly from your **computer into Canva** to upload them instantly.
✔ Use the **Layers Panel** (coming soon to Canva) to easily select and move items in complex designs.

---

3. Lesser-Known Shortcuts and Hacks

Canva has hidden shortcuts that can save you **tons of time**. Here are some **keyboard shortcuts** and **advanced tricks** to make designing faster.

Canva Keyboard Shortcuts

🖥 Basic Editing
- ✔ **Ctrl (Cmd) + C** → Copy
- ✔ **Ctrl (Cmd) + V** → Paste
- ✔ **Ctrl (Cmd) + D** → Duplicate
- ✔ **Ctrl (Cmd) + Z** → Undo
- ✔ **Ctrl (Cmd) + Shift + Z** → Redo

🖐 Design and Alignment
- ✔ **Alt (Option) + Drag** → Duplicate while dragging
- ✔ **Shift + Click** → Select multiple elements
- ✔ **L** → Insert a line
- ✔ **R** → Insert a rectangle
- ✔ **T** → Insert a text box

💡 Time-Saving Hacks
- ✔ **Magic Resize** (Pro feature) – Instantly resize your design for different platforms.

✔ **Remove Background** (Pro feature) – Instantly erase image backgrounds.

✔ **Use Smart Mockups** – Place your design on devices, T-shirts, or posters in one click.

◆ **Pro Tip:** Hold **Shift** while resizing to maintain **proportions**.

---

4. Staying Updated with Canva's Latest Features

Canva frequently **releases new features** to improve design capabilities. Staying updated ensures you're **using the latest tools and making the most out of Canva's potential**.

How to Stay Updated on Canva's New Features

✔ **Follow Canva's Blog** – Canva regularly updates its blog with new feature releases.

✔ **Join the Canva Community** – Participate in Canva Facebook groups and online forums.

✔ **Subscribe to Canva's YouTube Channel** –

Canva posts tutorials on using new tools.

✔ **Check the "What's New" Section in Canva** – Found in the dashboard for quick updates.

Recent Canva Features (2024 Updates)

✔ **AI-Powered Magic Write** – Canva's AI text generator for content creation.

✔ **Draw Tool** – Freehand drawing tool for custom illustrations.

✔ **Canva Websites** – Create one-page websites directly in Canva.

✔ **Text-to-Image AI Generator** – Converts text descriptions into AI-generated images.

✔ **Advanced Video Editing** – Canva now supports multi-layer video editing.

◆ **Pro Tip:** Experiment with new features early so you stay ahead of the competition!

Conclusion and Next Steps: Mastering Canva Beyond This Book

Congratulations! You've now explored **every essential feature and advanced function of Canva**—from getting started with the basics to designing professional-level graphics, collaborating with teams, and even monetizing your Canva skills. However, **learning never truly stops**. Canva is constantly evolving, and staying up to date with new tools, techniques, and trends is crucial to **unlocking your full creative potential**.

In this final chapter, we'll discuss:

1. **Continuing Your Learning Journey**
2. **Resources and Communities for Growth**
3. **Final Thoughts and Motivation**

---

1. Continuing Your Learning Journey

While this book has provided a **comprehensive guide** to Canva, the best way to **truly master the platform** is by continuous learning, experimentation, and real-world application. Here's how you can continue to grow as a Canva designer:

1. Stay Updated with Canva's New Features

Canva frequently **introduces new tools and improvements** to enhance user experience. By keeping up with these updates, you ensure that your designs remain modern and effective.

✔ **Check Canva's "What's New" Section** – Found on the Canva homepage, this area highlights newly released features.

✔ **Subscribe to Canva's Blog** – Canva regularly posts feature updates, design tips, and industry trends.

✔ **Follow Canva's YouTube Channel** – Canva's official channel provides **video tutorials** on new features.

◆ **Pro Tip:** Experiment with every new tool Canva releases—it could be the key to **enhancing your design efficiency**!

2. Practice, Experiment, and Create Daily

The best way to improve your Canva skills is **consistent practice**. Try these methods to develop your expertise:

✔ **Take on Small Design Challenges** – Design a **social media post**, flyer, or logo every day.

✔ **Recreate Professional Designs** – Browse **Pinterest, Behance, or Instagram**, and try to **replicate great designs** in Canva.

✔ **Redesign Old Projects** – Improve past designs with **new techniques** you've learned.

✔ **Explore Different Styles and Trends** – Experiment with **minimalist, bold, vintage, or futuristic designs**.

◆ **Pro Tip:** Set a **personal design project**—such as branding your own imaginary business—to **push your creativity**!

3. Specialize in a Design Niche

Once you're comfortable with Canva, you may want to **focus on a specific niche**. Specialization can make you **stand out in the industry and attract high-paying clients**.

✔ **Social Media Design** – Become an expert in Instagram, YouTube, LinkedIn, and Pinterest graphics.

✔ **Branding & Identity** – Master logo design, brand kits, and marketing collateral.

✔ **E-book and Course Design** – Create engaging workbooks, presentations, and e-learning materials.

✔ **Canva Template Seller** – Design and sell **pre-made templates** for passive income.

◆ **Pro Tip:** Check out Canva's **Design Trends Report** to see what's in demand and adapt your skills accordingly.

---

2. Resources and Communities for Growth

To **further your Canva journey**, you'll want to **connect with the right resources and communities**. These will help you **stay inspired, find solutions, and network with other designers**.

1. Canva Learning Resources

✔ **Canva Design School** – Canva offers **free online courses, tutorials, and design principles** to improve your skills.
✔ **Canva YouTube Channel** – A great place to find **step-by-step guides** on using advanced features.

✔ **Skillshare & Udemy** – Paid and free Canva courses available for in-depth learning.

2. Canva Communities and Forums

Joining a **community of designers** will expose you to **new ideas, design critiques, and business opportunities**.

✔ **Canva Design Circle (Facebook Group)** – The official Canva group where users share designs, ask questions, and get Canva updates.

✔ **Reddit (r/Canva)** – A forum where users discuss Canva tips, troubleshoot issues, and showcase designs.

✔ **Behance & Dribbble** – Platforms where designers share their work and get feedback.

✔ **LinkedIn Groups** – Canva-related groups for networking and learning from professionals.

◆ **Pro Tip:** Engage in these communities by **asking questions, sharing your work, and helping others**—you'll learn faster!

3. Inspiration & Design Idea Sources

✔ **Pinterest** – Find Canva design inspiration for **social media, branding, and marketing materials**.
✔ **Instagram Hashtags** – Follow #CanvaDesign, #GraphicDesign, and #CreativeEntrepreneur for design trends.
✔ **Canva Template Marketplace** – Explore professionally made Canva templates for ideas.

◆ **Pro Tip:** Start following **top Canva creators** to get inspiration and stay updated on design trends!

---

3. Final Thoughts and Motivation

As we reach the end of this book, remember: **Canva is a tool, but creativity is limitless.**

What You Have Achieved

🚀 **You've learned how to use Canva from scratch**—understanding everything from **basic navigation** to **advanced features**.
🧭 **You've mastered essential design**

skills—from **typography and color palettes** to **animations and video editing**.

💡 **You've unlocked Canva's full potential**—including **collaborating in teams, creating templates, and monetizing your skills**.

💰 **You've explored multiple income opportunities**—whether through **freelancing, selling templates, or running a design business**.

But this is just the beginning!

Your Next Steps

✔ **Start Your First Design Project** – Apply everything you've learned in a real project.

✔ **Join a Canva Challenge** – Participate in a **30-day design challenge** to improve your skills.

✔ **Monetize Your Skills** – If you're ready, start selling templates, offering freelance services, or launching a design-based business.

✔ **Teach Others** – The best way to master Canva is by helping othe uprs learn!

Bonus Hacks & Pro Tips for Canva Mastery

1. Hidden Canva Features You Probably Didn't Know

🔍 Secret Keyboard Shortcuts

Speed up your design process with these lesser-known **keyboard shortcuts**:

- **Press "C"** → Instantly add a circle
- **Press "L"** → Instantly add a line
- **Press "R"** → Instantly add a rectangle
- **Press "T"** → Instantly add a text box
- **Hold "Shift" + Drag** → Perfectly align objects while moving

- **Alt + Drag (Option on Mac)** → Instantly duplicate an element
- **Ctrl (Cmd) + G** → Group elements together
- **Ctrl (Cmd) + Shift + G** → Ungroup elements

◆ **Pro Tip:** Use **"Tidy Up" (Position > Tidy Up)** to perfectly align multiple elements in one click.

🎨 Color & Design Hacks

1. Create a Color Palette from an Image

Want to extract colors from an image?

✔ **Upload your image → Click on the color selector → Canva will generate a color palette from the image.**

2. Find Complementary Colors Easily

Not sure which colors look good together?

✔ Use **Canva's built-in color wheel**: Just select a color, and Canva will suggest matching shades.

◆ **Pro Tip:** Stick to **3-5 colors** for a clean, professional look.

📕 **Image & Background Tricks**

1. Remove Image Backgrounds (Without Canva Pro)

If you don't have Canva Pro, but need a transparent background:

✔ Use **Remove.bg** (a free online tool) to remove backgrounds, then upload the image back into Canva.

2. Turn Any Image into a Transparent Overlay

Want a **soft background effect** for text?

✔ Select an image → Click "Transparency" (checkerboard icon) → Reduce opacity to **50-70%**.

✏ Quick Design Enhancements

1. Instant Text Effects (Make Your Text Pop!)

✔ **Shadow Effect:** Click on text → Effects → Shadow → Adjust transparency and blur for a 3D effect.
✔ **Neon Glow Effect:** Click on text → Effects → Choose "Neon" → Adjust glow intensity.
✔ **Hollow Text:** Click on text → Effects → Splice → Set thickness to 100% → Adjust offset.

• **Pro Tip:** Use **text spacing (letter spacing + line height)** to improve readability.

📁 Organizing & Speeding Up Workflow

1. Save Time with Custom Templates

✔ If you create similar designs frequently, **save them as templates** (Click "File" → "Save as Template").

2. Organize Your Designs with Folders

✔ **Use folders to categorize designs** (Social Media, Business, Marketing, Personal).
✔ **Archive old designs** to keep your dashboard clean.

◆ **Pro Tip:** Name your files properly (e.g., "Instagram Story - Summer Sale" instead of "Untitled Design").

---

2. Monetization Bonus Tips (Make Money with Canva!)

💰 Ways to Make Money with Canva

1. Sell Canva Templates on Etsy or Creative Market

✔ Design **Instagram templates, eBook covers, Pinterest pins, planners, business cards** and sell them online.

✔ Use **Canva Pro** to create editable templates for buyers.

2. Start a Freelance Design Business

✔ Offer **social media graphics, branding kits, presentations, and business cards** on Fiverr or Upwork.

✔ Charge premium rates for **custom branding and marketing materials**.

3. Create a Print-on-Demand Business

✔ Design **T-shirts, mugs, posters, tote bags** and sell them on **Redbubble, Printful, or Teespring**.

✔ Use **Smart Mockups** in Canva to showcase products professionally.

• **Pro Tip:** Start by offering **a few free templates** to build an audience, then upsell premium designs.

---

3. Hidden Canva Features (That Most People Don't Use!)

◼ 1. Convert Designs into Mockups Instantly

✔ Upload your design → Click "Apps" → Search for **Smart Mockups** → Select a device or product.
✔ This works for **T-shirts, laptops, books, and posters!**

📹 2. Create Animated Videos in Canva

✔ Add elements → Click "Animate" → Choose **Slide, Fade, Pan, or Rise**.
✔ Export as **MP4** or **GIF**.

🌐 3. Make a Simple Website in Canva

✔ Canva now lets you design **one-page websites** (great for portfolios & landing pages!).
✔ Click "Share" → Select "Website" → Choose a layout.

Final Bonus: Canva Cheat Sheet!

Canva Best Practices for Pro-Level Designs

✔ **Use a maximum of 2 fonts** for readability.

✔ **Keep margins and spacing balanced** (don't overcrowd your design).

✔ **Align everything properly** (use guides & grids).

✔ **Use contrast** to make text readable against backgrounds.

✔ **Use high-quality images** (avoid pixelation).

Canva Glossary: Terms & Definitions

A

Alignment – A design principle that helps organize elements evenly (left, right, center, or justified). Canva provides auto-alignment tools.

Animations – Motion effects that can be applied to text, images, and elements to create engaging videos and presentations.

Aspect Ratio – The proportional relationship between an image's width and height (e.g., 16:9 for YouTube thumbnails, 1:1 for Instagram posts).

Apps & Integrations – Third-party tools that work within Canva, such as **Google Drive, Pexels, Giphy, and Smart Mockups**.

B

Background Remover – A Canva Pro tool that instantly removes the background from an image.

Brand Kit – A Canva Pro feature that allows you to **store and apply brand colors, fonts, and logos** to maintain consistency.

Bleed – Extra space around a design that ensures full coverage when printing (Canva provides a "show bleed" option for professional print designs).

C

Canva Print – A feature that allows users to order high-quality prints of their designs, including business cards, flyers, and invitations.

Crop – Trimming or resizing an image to focus on a specific area.

Color Palette Generator – A Canva tool that extracts colors from an uploaded image to create a custom color scheme.

Collaboration – The ability to share and edit designs with team members in real time.

Copy Style – A quick tool that allows users to copy the formatting (colors, fonts, styles) from one element to another.

D

Dashboard – The main screen where you access all of your projects, templates, and design tools.

Drag & Drop – The method of **adding elements, images, and text by dragging them onto the design canvas**.

Download Options – Canva allows you to download designs in **PNG, JPG, PDF, MP4, GIF, and SVG formats**.

E

Elements – Shapes, icons, lines, illustrations, and stickers available in Canva's library.

Effects – Modifications that can be applied to text and images, such as **shadows, glows, and neon text styles**.

Embed – A feature that allows you to insert Canva designs into websites without downloading them.

F

Frames – Shapes that allow images to be **clipped into a specific shape** (e.g., circles, laptops, or letters).

Filters – Image adjustments that enhance brightness, contrast, and saturation.

Font Pairing – Canva suggests **matching font combinations** to create visually appealing typography.

G

Grid – A layout tool that helps **align elements properly** for a clean and organized design.

Gradient – A smooth transition between two or more colors used as backgrounds or overlays.

H

Hyperlink – In Canva's PDF designs, users can **add clickable links to text and images**.

I

Image Adjustments – Tools that let you edit brightness, contrast, blur, and transparency.

Illustrations – Hand-drawn or digital drawings available in Canva's elements library.

K

Keyboard Shortcuts – Quick key combinations that speed up design tasks (e.g., "T" for text, "L" for line).

L

Layers – The arrangement of elements in a design. Canva does not have a full layering system like Photoshop, but you can **move elements forward or backward**.

Lock Feature – Prevents an element from being accidentally moved or edited.

M

Magic Resize – A Canva Pro feature that **instantly resizes designs** for different formats (e.g., turning a Facebook post into an Instagram Story).

Margins – The spacing around text and images to improve readability and balance.

Mockups – Realistic previews that place designs onto **T-shirts, laptops, mugs, and more**.

N

Neon Effect – A text effect that gives a glowing, neon-style look.

Nudge – Using the arrow keys to move elements in small increments for precise alignment.

O

Opacity – Adjusts how transparent or solid an element appears.

Outline Effect – A text effect that creates a hollow look around letters.

P

PNG (Portable Network Graphics) – A **high-quality image format that supports transparency**, ideal for social media posts and logos.

PDF (Portable Document Format) – Used for **printing documents and presentations**. Canva supports **standard PDFs and PDF Print**.

Presentation Mode – A feature that allows users to **present their slides directly from Canva**.

Publish – The option to share or export designs to social media, websites, or as downloadable files.

R

Rulers & Guides – Helps align elements properly to maintain consistency in design.

Resize (Pro Feature) – Lets you **change the dimensions of a design instantly** without recreating it from scratch.

S

Shadow Effect – An effect that creates depth behind text and objects.

Stock Photos – A **built-in library of free and premium images** available for use in designs.

SVG (Scalable Vector Graphics) – A **vector format that allows resizing without losing quality** (available only in Canva Pro).

Styles – Pre-made **color and font combinations** that can be applied to a design.

Smart Mockups – A tool that **places your design into a real-world scene** (e.g., displaying a logo on a T-shirt).

T

Templates – Pre-designed layouts that can be customized for different projects like social media, presentations, and business cards.

Text Effects – Options like **curve, glitch, neon, and shadow** to enhance typography.

Transparency – Adjusting an element's opacity to make it **more or less visible**.

U

Upload – The feature that lets users add **custom images, fonts, and videos** to their designs.

Undo/Redo – **Ctrl + Z (Cmd + Z on Mac) to undo, Ctrl + Shift + Z (Cmd + Shift + Z on Mac) to redo**.

V

Video Editing Tools – Canva allows users to **trim, cut, and animate videos** for social media and presentations.

Version History – Canva Pro users can **restore previous versions of a design**.

W

Watermark – A faint text or logo that appears over a design (Canva applies this to premium elements until they are purchased).

Website Builder – A feature in Canva that lets users create **one-page websites** easily.

White Space – The empty space around design elements to **improve readability and focus**.

Z

Zoom – Used to **enlarge or shrink the design canvas** for detailed editing.

Ultimate Canva Manual

Ultimate Canva Manual

www.ingramcontent.com/pod-product-compliance
Lightning Source LLC
LaVergne TN
LVHW051243050326
832903LV00028B/2544